IF YOU ONLY HAD SIX MONTHS TO LIVE, WHAT WOULD YOU DO?

DR. ALEKSANDER ŠINIGOJ

INCLUDES A FREE
INSPIRATIONAL MIND PROGRAMMING
RECORDING (DOWNLOAD)

THE BOOK THAT CAN TURN YOUR VALUES UPSIDE DOWN

If you only had six months to live, what would you do?

Dr. Aleksander Šinigoj

ISBN-13: 978-1500683559

The trouble is,
you think
you have time.

BUDDHA

DISCLAIMER

This book is intended as an inspiration or motivation for anyone who would like to find true meaning and true values in life. Neither the author nor the publisher assume any responsibility for any errors or omissions, nor do they represent or warrant that the information, ideas, plans, actions, suggestions, and/or methods of operation contained herein are in all cases true, accurate, appropriate, or legal. It is the reader's responsibility to consult with his or her own advisor, or an expert for a specific area before putting any of the enclosed information, plans, examples, ideas, or practices into play. The author encourages the reader to consult with a specific expert before implementing any changes in hierarchy of values and acting upon it. The book includes a link to a free mind programming recording. The author and the publisher specifically disclaim any liability resulting from the application of the information contained in this book or application of the actual recording. The information or any of the ideas are not intended to serve as legal advice related to individual situations.

All of the research, along with the entire book, is based on the author's experiences and opinions. The author's model of the world, his values, beliefs and thinking processes represent limitations, which should be taken into account when reading the book. Further studying, skills and competencies and expert opinions should be taken into consideration before any action is taken.

Life is really
simple, but we
insist on making it
complicated.

CONFUCIUS

Contents

DEDICATION

I want to dedicate this book to my family. For their love and support.

And I want to dedicate this book also to you my dear reader. There are no coincidences. It is not a coincidence you have this book in front of you to read.

Life is short.

And the time limit that we have in this life is something that tells us that we should not waste our time and our lives by living someone else's life.

Find what you love doing, find what is truly important to you, not what others think and believe, but what you believe in your heart. Be happy and find your inner peace. You deserve to be happy and peaceful.

When you came into this world, you were happy and peaceful. But along your journey you might have forgotten how to be happy. Perhaps this book can remind you about what you can do more and what less, what to eliminate from your life and what to keep, from whom to ask forgiveness and whom to forgive, but most importantly, how to enjoy every single moment of your life.

My prayer, which I am doing right now, (and I literally stopped writing for a few moments) is that you live your life as who you truly are, that you find strength, courage, and the capability, to enjoy life with all your heart. That you would love and appreciate yourself more. My prayer for you is to have a magnificent life, life that would be the life that you might not even dare to dream.

That you would commit to do whatever it takes to feel good. Harm no one, not others, not yourself. Wish everyone love, joy and happiness, but focus on yourself. What do you want for yourself at your core? How can you feel good? What is truly important to you? Find answers to those questions and remember to be happy. Your inner guidance will help you. Look and find unlimited ways to get happy. From today on, until the end of time.

Thus, I dedicate this book to you. May you find with the exercises, examples and questions those which will help you define and decide what is truly important to you. Listen to your heart more. Follow your dreams and have a magnificent life, full of joy and happiness.

You have my love and my support.
To your happiness,
Dr. Aleksander Šinigoj

In the long run
we are all dead.

JOHN MAYNARD KEYNES

THE JOURNEY

I am dying. So are you.

I am not sure how much time I still have to live. You probably don't know that either. I hope and I wish you have many, many years, many decades to live and enjoy life. But there is a limit for me and for you in this body in this dimension, whatever you decide to believe or not to believe.

My dream and desired goal is to live happily and healthily until 13th of October 2081 when I will be 107 years old (remember to send me a birthday card). Although I have a written goal I am still not sure if the Universe will listen to my goal or not.

And even if the Universe or God might listen to my prayer and wishes, either way I will be dead the next day, on 14th of October 2081. So I am dying for sure. At least in this body and in this form of life where I am right now.

And so are you. This body and this form of life have unfortunately a limit for you, too. You are also dying, and you know it. You may not think about it often, but one day it will happen. And you can decide today to live happily and healthily many more decades and for many more years to come.

But one day your time will also come, and you know it.

People like to joke that there are two things that are certain, death and taxes. No matter how old you are and how smart you are or how much money you have in your bank account, you are dying, maybe not just yet, but one day.

And that is great, it is how it is supposed to be. The meaning of death can help us think about what is really important in life. To stop rushing through our lives.

Death and the awareness that we are all dying can help us focus on our lives with a sense of gratitude and awareness of every single moment that we are here. We begin to want more from life, to stop wasting precious time. So my journey, which will hopefully soon also become your journey, is to look at how you can be happier, how you can enjoy life more. And this book has been written to help people become aware of that. To understand that they have only a certain number of holidays, birthday celebrations, and festive days, and that they should focus on enjoying them. Being happy. Being present.

I have been writing this book for a very long time, years. I have changed the title over and over again. I also changed the content again and again. The version that you are now reading is completely different from the original version. And like I have done many times, I started writing another book and finished it in the meantime. I also started writing other books and haven't finished them yet, as well. But this book and the energy associated with this book, the whole message behind the actual book has recently become so strong and on my mind so much, I felt the urge to finish it. To give it to you to read it and experience it. I do not even think I wrote it myself. I think there was a special and strange force of the Universe or God or whatever you might call it that is actually helped me to write. And the message is for you, my dear reader. Change your life for the better.

There are several exercises, examples and questions in this

book. I have done these exercises you are about to read in the book on myself and with my students several times. I have used them in different workshops and I adjust them to the people and according to the content of the workshop.

It always amazes me how powerful all those exercises are.

After a full week of life changing experience at one particular training, where people truly felt inspired and motivated, one of the participants came to me and told me that the exercises and questions, which are now part of this book, were so powerful and life changing for him, that they were worth much more than he paid for the workshop.

And I was the first to try those exercises on myself. Before I run things in my training workshops, I like to experience them. To me, the questions and exercises within are some of most powerful ones that I have experienced in my life. I have been through so many different changes in my life, from small ones that you might find so simple and so unimportant, to huge ones. I will spend some time later on discussing some of those changes with you, but let me first talk to you about my journey.

I have spent much time and money studying and learning. Reading books, attending workshops and seminars, practicing and learning from my mistakes. Many experiences that I came upon in my life were not pleasant to me at all, but they helped me grow and become better, wiser, and brought me back to my core values.

In the trainings I have attended as a participant, I have done many powerful exercises. For my own trainings, which I have been running and doing in the last few decades, I invented many new exercises and used several powerful questions. I have done many powerful exercises, but the one that I am about to do is one of the most powerful ones. It focuses people on thinking about what is truly important in their lives. Are they living lives that are their own, or lives programmed and designed by other people?

It is always about some excuse or story that they will tell you, why they cannot start living for real yet. Their family member, wife, husband, not enough time, not enough education, bad economy, etc. And you can listen to those excuses for ages. And perhaps you can talk about why you do not yet have the career, money, relationships, health, fitness, joy, happiness in your life.

Or you can stop for a moment. I invite you to this journey to experience a different view of your life, to look at your life with a different set of priorities, which is called 'a different hierarchy of values.' Take this journey while you are reading this book as an experimental journey, to see, hear and feel how your life will be different if you had a different 'hierarchy of values.'

There are only two
ways to live your
life. One is as though
nothing is a miracle.
The other is as
though everything is
a miracle.

ALBERT EINSTEIN

A SQUARE STAKE STORY

Before we start, let me offer a metaphor that I like to use in my workshops. I heard it some time ago, I cannot remember from whom, and very likely you have heard it in some other form, perhaps in a slightly different format. The story is about a young woman who married a young handsome doctor. He was a perfect match for her. They loved each other very much and they were happy together. After they married, the new bride moved into his house, where the doctor's mother also lived. Fortunately for the bride, her new mother-in-law was a nice, charming old lady.

The two connected well at first, until the young wife started cooking. One day, she took meat from the freezer and cut the steaks in squares. While she was doing that, she threw away lots of good, tasty meat. For a while the mother-in-law calmly watched the young bride, but in her heart and in her mind she was angry about all the wasted meat that her son's wife was creating. A few weeks later, when her daughter-in-law threw away some special turkey steak pieces, she became furious and screamed, "Why do you cut the stakes in squares? Why do you throw away so much good and tasty meat?"

The new bride replied, "Because my mother taught me to do that, all our family cuts the meat that way. It is the right thing to do in order to have the best and tastiest experience. The other meat is tasteless."

They soon started arguing, each fighting for their own beliefs and fighting for their own rights. The young doctor stood between his new bride and his mother, trying to calm them down. After so many weeks and months of fighting the young couple decided to visit the wife's mother, looking for the real cause of cutting the steaks in squares and throwing the meat away. The wife's mother sent them to her grandmother telling them the same story that the young bride told. And the grandmother remembered that her mother taught them to cut the meat in squares because their pans were small and square, and the only way the meat could fit in the pan was by cutting it. She could not remember why they did not use the remaining meat, but that was how she was raised and that felt right.

The whole idea behind the story is that we come into this world without any value hierarchy, beliefs, strategies; we learn them. We learned much from our parents and from our teachers and from our experiences and now as adults we have thousands and thousands of beliefs, which help us get through our lives easier but also make our lives complicated and not so easy. Once we have played with fire and burned ourselves, it is good if we do not repeat that as we know that when playing with fire we can get burned. However, when we need to prepare a meal and we need fire to do that, that particular belief could be a limiting belief.

It is the same with values. Sometimes we procrastinate and delay activities simply based on our value hierarchy. Acting upon what is important in our lives and acting or finishing activities and expressing our true feelings and our true identity might simply be based on our beliefs and values that we have. A simple change in that value system and beliefs could lead to a different behavior and, as we say, to a completely different life. The book and exercises are not meant to point out and solve limitations that you might have based on your current hierarchy of values. If you believe that you have some limitations that you need to work upon, I would encourage you to deal with them. Value and beliefs are very important because they influence your behavior and your behavior is what produces the results in your life. But for the actual purpose of this book, it is enough that you acknowledge and understand that you have certain beliefs and values, and by changing those values your life can change.

The idea behind the book is that you will start living your own life, living a life with a purpose, being happier. Start living your life the way you want and desire. Stop cutting the meat in squares because someone told you to. Start cutting the meat or start living your live based on what your heart desires and based on what you would like to be, have and do. You are the creator of your life. Perhaps you have lived based on old patterns, old limitations, but now it is time to change. You are reading this book because it is time to change your programs.

When I look back on all these worries, I remember the story of the old man who said on his deathbed that he had had a lot of trouble in his life, most of which had never happened.

WINSTON CHURCHILL

THERE IS NO RIGHT OR WRONG WAY TO DO THIS

I am about to offer what I think is a good way to go through this book and work on the exercises. You might do this in a different way. There is no right or wrong, it is up to you how you want to do the exercises. The most important thing is that you are honest with yourself. That you stop listening to your mind and open your heart; your heart knows what is truly most important to you and what you would like to change, experience, and implement in your life.

In the next chapter we will start with our questions and some exercises. I would recommend you do the exercises in a place and time where you will not be disturbed. To do them thoroughly it is recommended to take at least 30 minutes of your time. However, if you take a couple of hours or even a full day, it will be much, much better. It is up to you. When I first did this exercise I went for a long walk to a place deep in a forest, to a place where I knew I wouldn't be disturbed. Switch off your phone and all other distractions. Remember, this is your life.

Do your best, be curious and make sure you do not think too much when answering questions and doing the exercises.

And do not do this only by reading and repeating the answers in your mind. Write the answers down in the book. By actually writing answers down, you will experience this exercise in a different way. You will feel it and experience it not only in your mind, but also in your body. The same process on which you are about to embark I teach to my coaching students. It is truly a remarkable coaching tool. And if you are a coach, you can use the process, or some specific parts of it, for your clients.

When you start the exercises remember to do them quickly. Write them down as fast as you can. Sometimes I write so fast that I cannot read my own handwriting afterwards, but I know that the answers are in my body, I experienced them when I was writing them. These exercises are about speed, the faster you do them, the better the results will be. Speed does not mean that you do not take time to actually experience what you are feeling during a particular exercise. Speed means that you have written down whatever had come to your mind. Some questions have been asked again and again. Answer them even if you feel you are repeating yourself, as you will be answering them from a different time perspective. We reserved enough space in the book for you to write, and we encourage you to use the book so that many months or even years in the future you will be able to look back at the book in order to see what you have since learned, In case there is not enough space, use additional paper or write anyplace in the book where there is available space. The moment you write something in the book, you become a co-creator of the book, a co-creator of this experience.

I would encourage you to do these exercises at least once a year if not more often, so that you will know whether or not you are on the right track. I am deeply touched and moved that you decided to go on this incredible journey that can change your life forever. Thank you.

Have no fear, the book and the story has a happy ending.

I think that is it.

Are you ready and excited?

Let's begin.

The fear of death follows from the fear of life. A man who lives fully is prepared to die at any time.

MARK TWAIN

IF YOU ONLY HAD SIX MONTHS TO LIVE?

Imagine this hypothetical limitation that has been imposed on you:

- you only have six months to live,
- you cannot tell anyone,
- you will be completely healthy for the full six months,
- you cannot extend nor buy any extra time,
- your current situation, your financial situation, your job, family, whatever you currently have or do stays the same, nothing else changes, unless you make it so in the last six months that you have, but at the beginning you are where you are.

Remember the rules, as they are really important, so if you give any clues to anyone, or tell this to someone, you will be gone in a heartbeat; you will disappear from this planet the very moment you talk to anyone about this. You will be completely healthy all six months, but you cannot extend nor buy any extra time as many people say they will fight for more time. You have no extra money in your account for this game. These are the simple rules. Only six months to live, no extra time, you cannot tell this to anyone. I hope it is clear, so that you can begin writing now. Please write as much as you can, write quickly and at the same time take your time to experience the learning of the exercise and remember that this exercise is actually about writing.

Some of the answers and exercises might be applicable for you, some not. Do all or as many as you can. Go for the ones that resonate with you, the exercises you will find most powerful.

If you were faced with this idea,
how would your life change?

What would you do first, second, third etc?

What would become more important to you,
what less?

_____

_____

_____

_____

_____

_____

_____

_____

_____

_____

_____

_____

_____

_____

What would you want to create during that time?

_____

_____

_____

_____

_____

_____

_____

_____

_____

_____

_____

_____

_____

_____

_____

_____

_____

What activities would you start doing that you had been postponing for a long time?

_____

_____

_____

_____

_____

_____

_____

_____

_____

_____

_____

_____

_____

_____

What activities would you stop doing?

Who would you like to spend more time with?

_____

_____

_____

_____

_____

_____

_____

_____

_____

_____

_____

_____

_____

_____

_____

Who would you like to spend less time with?

Who would you like to forgive and from whom you would like to ask forgiveness?

What would you like to tell to the people that you love?

_____

_____

_____

_____

_____

_____

_____

_____

_____

_____

_____

_____

_____

_____

_____

If there was something that people would say about you, what would they say about your last six months?

_____

_____

_____

_____

_____

_____

_____

_____

_____

_____

_____

_____

_____

_____

What are you most grateful for?

What would be one sentence, one sentence that would express what you would like to communicate to the people that you love, perhaps to all the children in the world that start to experience this thing called life, perhaps to your grandchildren or great grandchildren that you will never meet?

What are the 13 key things to do, see, hear, feel, experience, enjoy in the last six months of your life? If you have more than 13, please use extra space.

1. _____

2. _____

3. _____

4. _____

5. _____

6. _____

7. _____

8. _____

9. _____

10. _____

11. _____

12. _____

13. _____

Remembering that I'll be dead soon is the most important tool I've ever encountered to help me make the big choices in life. Because almost everything - all external expectations, all pride, all fear of embarrassment or failure - these things just fall away in the face of death, leaving only what is truly important.

STEVE JOBS

IF YOU ONLY HAD ONE MONTH TO LIVE?

Now the rules of the game have changed. Forget about the previous exercise, so you actually have only one month to live and not six months. How much difference would that make in your life? Would you continue doing what you are doing? What is the difference between one and six months? How would your life be different? So many times one month goes by really quickly. A single month allows you to travel and allows you to visit some places around the world. You may also want to spend some time working or simply quit if you do not love what you do. You can have plenty of time to spend it with your loved ones and still leave some time to be on your own, in nature, doing what you love most. There is enough time to leave a note or a message or even to write a real book that would inform, inspire or help other people. There is still plenty of time, but in reality there is not so much time. If you only had one month to live, what would you do?

Who would you like to spend more time with?

Who would you like to spend less time with?

What would be important for you to feel in the last month of your life?

What message would you like to communicate to the people you love during the last month of your life?

_____

_____

_____

_____

_____

_____

_____

_____

_____

_____

_____

_____

_____

_____

What would you like to see or visit during the last month of your life?

What kind of a diet would you like to eat during the last month of your life?

_____

_____

_____

_____

_____

_____

_____

_____

_____

_____

_____

_____

_____

_____

_____

What would you like for others to say about the last month of your life?

_____

_____

_____

_____

_____

_____

_____

_____

_____

_____

_____

_____

_____

_____

_____

How much time would you like to spend working in
the last month of your life?

_____

_____

_____

_____

_____

_____

_____

_____

_____

_____

_____

_____

_____

_____

It is not the end of
the physical body that
should worry us.
Rather, our concern
must be to live while
we're alive - to release
our inner selves from
the spiritual death that
comes with living behind
a facade designed to
conform to external
definitions of who and
what we are.

ELISABETH KUBLER-ROSS

IF YOU ONLY HAD ONE WEEK TO LIVE?

The rules change, again. Forget about previous exercises. There is no more one month, there is only one week. All the other rules stay the same, the only change is that now you have less time. Is there something different from one month to one week? Do you have a favorite day of the week? Some people really love Friday afternoons, some people love Saturdays or Sundays. Some people hate Mondays. Now you will have a chance to experience, for the last time, every single day of the week. How much time will you sleep during that last week? Planning your activities could be truly important or you can simply take every day as it comes. You might not be able to travel far away to visit as many places as you could visit in six months or in one month, but you can still have some traveling experiences in a single week. Imagine that you can write a short book or a short story that would be left behind to the people that you love. And you can set your affairs in order. You might want to taste some different foods. Enjoy life. Hug, love and smile at the world. Experience the gratitude of being alive for the last week, being grateful for every single moment. It sounds like so little or it sounds like so much. Some people do not have a week; they are unfortunately not informed about when they will die, so you can consider this as a privilege. If you only had one week to live, what would you really do?

How important is your job in this last week? How much time would you like to spend working during the last week?

What would you like to see, visit, or experience?

Who would you like to spend more time with?

What would you like to tell to the people that you love?

_____

_____

_____

_____

_____

_____

_____

_____

_____

_____

_____

_____

_____

_____

Is there a particular message you would like to give to the rest of the world?

Life is what happens
to you while you're
busy making other
plans.

ALLEN SAUNDERS

IF YOU ONLY HAD ONE DAY TO LIVE?

Again the rules change. There is no longer six months, no longer one month, there is no longer one week. You only have one day, you only have 24 hours to live. One day really includes one sunrise and one sunset. Just one. And, of course, you can see the sun only if there are no clouds. If this last day of your life would be a sunny day, you might not see, hear or feel the rain again. Can you remember how many wonderful sunrises and sunsets have gone by, without you even noticing or enjoying them? A single day leaves you, perhaps, with enough time to visit the people you love and to hug them for the last time. A single day leaves you with very limited time; you might not be able to travel far. One day gives you only a few good meals to eat, understanding that you might not want too much food or too much of your energy being consumed by the food you eat. In your mind imagine how you would like to live that last day. By having so little time, what would now be truly important? If you only had one day to live, what would you do?

What would you like to do on that last day of your life?

Who would you like to spend that time with?

What kind of a car would you like to drive?

Whom would like to express gratitude to?

_____

_____

_____

_____

_____

_____

_____

_____

_____

_____

_____

_____

_____

_____

Is there a special message you would like to express to a one particular person? What would that message be?

What would be the message to your loved ones?
Do you have a particular message for certain
people?

_____

_____

_____

_____

_____

_____

_____

_____

_____

_____

_____

_____

_____

_____

_____

What are the best memories that you would like to
remember in the last day of your life?

What would you like to watch on TV the last day of
your life?

_____

_____

_____

_____

_____

_____

_____

_____

_____

_____

_____

_____

_____

_____

_____

How much time would you like to spend working and what job activities would you like to do on the last day of your life?

Don't cry because it's over, smile because it happened.

DR. SEUSS

IF YOU ONLY HAD ONE HOUR TO LIVE?

What if you do not have even a day? What if you only have a single hour? Sixty minutes? There are really so many things you can see, visit or actually experience in that last hour. You can have a tasty meal and spend some time with your loved ones. You can write a letter or record a video with a message that will remain for the people you cherish and love. You can invite over friends and family, those who are nearby might reach you in that hour, but you will need to find a good excuse to spend time together. Or you might retire to a place in nature, to a place where you will be all by yourself. In that last day, you may wish to remember the best memories of your life. Experience the smell of grass and trees. Experience every single breath you will take in that last hour. Think about it: If you only had one hour to live, what would you do?

How would that change what is truly important in your life?

What would you do if you only had one hour to live?

With whom would you want to spend that hour?

What kind of a car would like you to have in your garage?

How much money would you like to have in your bank account?

What kind of food would you like to eat in that last hour?

_____

_____

_____

_____

_____

_____

_____

_____

_____

_____

_____

_____

_____

Is there a particular TV show that you would like to watch during the last hour of your life?

_____

_____

_____

_____

_____

_____

_____

_____

_____

_____

_____

_____

_____

_____

What would you like other people to think about you during the last hour of your life?

_____

_____

_____

_____

_____

_____

_____

_____

_____

_____

_____

_____

_____

_____

What would you like to tell the people you love
in the last hour of your life?

_____

_____

_____

_____

_____

_____

_____

_____

_____

_____

_____

_____

_____

_____

_____

The world is not imperfect or slowly evolving along a path to perfection. No, it is perfect at every moment.

Herman Hesse

IF YOU ONLY HAD ONE MINUTE TO LIVE?

One hour really sounded like so little. If you have a big family, you might not even be able to tell everyone that you love them and hug them before leaving this world. Of course, you are still not allowed to tell them the whole truth: You are dying. But simply express love, appreciation and wish them all the best. What if you do not have even an hour? What if you only have a single minute? Sixty seconds? It sounds so short, but that is what life is made of. Seconds, minutes. And now you only have a single minute to live. You know that many times in reality, people are not given that special minute, to reflect, to think, to be present. To find that special feeling of enlightenment for the very last time. To finally understand what is truly important in life. To be fully present and experience every single second there is left. Can you imagine that you only have one single minute to live? If you only had a minute to live, what would you do?

How would that change what is important in
your life?

What would you do if you only had one minute to live?

IF YOU ONLY HAD ONE MINUTE TO LIVE?

How would you want to spend that minute?

98

What kind of a car would you like to have in your garage in the last minute of your life?

What kind of clothes would you like to be wearing?

What kind of house would you like to be living in?

How much money would you like to have in your bank account?

What would you like to eat in that last minute?

What would be your last words of wisdom?

What would you like to feel during that last minute?

To whom would you like to express love?

Is there a special memory that you would like to remember?

_____

_____

_____

_____

_____

_____

_____

_____

_____

_____

_____

_____

_____

_____

_____

Is there a person or persons that you would like to hug for the last time?

Is there someone from whom you would like to ask forgiveness? What words would you like to use? Whom would you like to forgive? What words would you use to forgive in the last moments of your life?

If there was a last sentence you would say to this world, to the people that are left behind, what would those words be?

If you would say the very last words of gratitude for your life, for whatever you have experienced so far, what would you say?

For death is no more than a turning of us over from time to eternity.

WILLIAM PENN

NOW YOU ARE GONE

Imagine that you have passed away. You just died. Peaceful-ly. Your last breath, your last thought in that particular body. Your body is left there, but your essence, your soul, your con-sciousness, whatever you wish to call it, has now left your body. You are observing your body there and you can move freely, watching others experiencing your death. How does it feel to be dead? Are you sad watching other people grieve? Do you have any regrets? Being dead, you left all your attach-ments, all your bad feelings behind in the old body. How does it feel to have peace and make peace with the world? Wouldn't be nicer if you had done all that already while you were alive. Looking from a distance and observing, how many worries, how much anger and other negative emotions you used to have and they were completely useless? How does it feel to finally understand that everything that happened in your life was love, that you were loved all along? Imagine in your mind what your loved ones would do after you die.

What happens around you and your dead body?

How do people feel now that you are gone? Who are the people that you have mostly touched?

_____

_____

_____

_____

_____

_____

_____

_____

_____

_____

_____

_____

_____

_____

_____

_____

NOW YOU ARE GONE

What does your funeral look like?

118

What do they read or say aloud at your funeral?

What do the attendees really think about you
in their hearts, but they do not say aloud at the
funeral?

Do you have any regrets in your life? Do you wish
you would have done something differently?

_____

_____

_____

_____

_____

_____

_____

_____

_____

_____

_____

_____

_____

_____

To live in hearts we
leave behind is not to
die.

THOMAS CAMPBELL

A FUTURE WITHOUT YOU

So many times we are obsessed with our work or even believe that no one else can do a job as well as we do it; so we spend time, energy and lots of effort on our everyday tasks and jobs. We believe ourselves irreplaceable. We think that we must do this, we must do that, or there will be consequences. We believe so strongly that the world would stop without us or that the world would not be the same without our strong influence. That our presence and our work and our impact is so important. We might be restless or simply forgetting to enjoy the moment because we are worrying that things are not getting done in our jobs or things are not getting done in our homes. Any yet, one day, we will leave our lives and leave our bodies and stop doing all that work. We will stop worrying and stop all our attachments on this planet. Imagine how this day looks. You are no longer there. Who is looking after your affairs? How does your family cope? Do they have the right values, right vision and right inner guidance to live their lives fully? Do they know that you loved them and you want them to be happy? Do they love themselves? You told them this so many times, but you also showed them with your deeds. Imagine the future without you. One year, ten years, twenty years, fifty years, one hundred years, two hundred years into the future after you have passed away. How does this future look without you?

How does the future look without you? What is missing in this world? How could the world be better if you were there?

What did you leave behind? What is your legacy?

_____

_____

_____

_____

_____

_____

_____

_____

_____

_____

_____

_____

_____

_____

How much better are the lives of people that were
close to you because of what you said, what you
were, who you were? What kind of example have
you been for them?

Look at the world from a distance. What have you left to this planet, to the people, to nature, to the Mother Earth?

If your life was a message, what message did you offer in life?

_____

_____

_____

_____

_____

_____

_____

_____

_____

_____

_____

_____

_____

_____

_____

Look into the future many, many years. Can you imagine how important your problems, your every day worries, would be 200 years into the future?

How is life without you some years in the future?

Every moment of your life is infinitely creative and the universe is endlessly bountiful. Just put forth a clear enough request, and everything your heart desires must come to you.

MAHATMA GANDHI

WHAT WOULD YOU CHANGE IF YOU HAD ANOTHER CHANCE?

Remember that you cannot change the past. The past is over. You can change the present and thus influence the future to be different. If a magic force would give you another chance, if your life would be suddenly and magically extended, given back to you, how would you live differently? Think about your career, your finances, your health, your relationships, your personal growth, your contribution to this planet and other areas that are important to you. Think about daring. Think about living up to your full potential. Think about acting and living as if you knew you could not fail. Think about living your dream life and being truly happy, healthy and grateful every single moment of your life. Think about being peaceful. Think about what you always wanted to be, have and do. What changes would you introduce into your life so that you would earn another opportunity? What changes will you introduce into your life based on the exercises you did before?

If I would be given another opportunity, another life,
I would more...

If I would be given another opportunity, another life, I would less...

If I would be given another opportunity, another life, I would no longer...

If I were given another opportunity, another life, I would start...

_____

_____

_____

_____

_____

_____

_____

_____

_____

_____

_____

_____

_____

_____

_____

_____

If I would be given another opportunity, another life,
I would love...

If I would be given another opportunity, another life,
I would tell...

If I would be given another opportunity, another life, I would learn...

If I would be given another opportunity, another life, I would be grateful for...

If I would be given another opportunity, another life, I would...

If I would be given another opportunity, another life, I wouldn't...

If I would be given another opportunity, another life, I would dare to...

Look back at the changes that you have written about to do. What is the one major change or shift in your life that would actually deserve a new life? Pick just one.

_____

_____

_____

_____

_____

_____

_____

_____

_____

_____

_____

_____

_____

_____

_____

If you could have another life, an ideal life, what other specific changes, beside the major change that you described previously, would you introduce into your life?

Don't die with your
music still in you.

WAYNE DYER

CONGRATULATIONS, YOU JUST GOT YOURSELF A NEW LIFE

Well done. Whatever you have written or not written in the previous chapter, you have been awarded another life. I am not sure how many books you have read that gave you another life. Well, this is a bonus, an extra gift in the book. A special surprise mentioned on the cover of this book. Your new life. I am not sure how much time you have spent filling in the exercises in this book so far, but if you went through them and felt them for real, you might have been touched at a particular time. Possibly, you had a different perspective on your perceived priorities. Please be aware that even without this book and all the exercises, every single moment is an opportunity for a new birth, every single moment is a true opportunity to start a new life. Every single moment offers you the opportunity to change your life, and your life will be different as a result of your decisions. This book might help you shift your values, but you can also do that yourself by listening to your inner voice and to your heart. Live your life the way you desire. Now that you can change your life and you have another opportunity, think about your new decisions, your new values, and your new activities. It is time to plan and design your new life. Remember, this is YOUR life.

As a part of new perspectives and new important values in your life, what are the three most important specific decisions you will commit to, being grateful for your new life?

What specific, measurable goals, stated positively, will you set for your new life? Set short and long term goals to do whatever you would like to be, have, do, achieve, live. And remember to go for it. You have received this special gift, a new life, but even though you have this new life, there is no time to waste. Enjoy it now, take advantage of it now, live to your full potential now. Now is the time.

Dare to be different. Represent your maker well and you will forever abide in the beautiful embrace of his loving arms.

JAACHYNMA N.E. AGU

WHAT OTHER PEOPLE DECIDED TO DO AFTER THESE EXERCISES

Below you will find some ideas from others. They came from several people that attended my workshops and from talking to many people about the book. Please use these ideas simply to gather your thoughts about what you will actually decide to do. I have no real statistics and I cannot give you a percentage of people that would make a certain decision or action if they were faced with the different scenarios in the book. If you like any of the ideas, you can add them to your action list. Listen to your heart when selecting new ideas.

A significant percentage of the people would quit their job. Some people would continue to do what they do because they love what they do. But all of them said they would not work so hard. They would work less and they would become more effective and focused when working. There is no doubt that a huge majority of people would spend less time working and more time with people and doing things they truly love. Work would become less important. People, feelings, being present, would be more important. I am mentioning this because people actually spend a lot of time at work, stressing, worrying etc., but when asked this question this particular issue becomes much less important.

However, I urge you not to quit your job overnight. You probably need to pay bills, and you need to eat. It is a good idea to first create a plan, to have a backup, before making any major decisions. But if you would quit your job if you only had six months to live, don't waste any time. Examine what you could do for a living, something that you like or truly love doing. What do you enjoy doing so much you would want to continue doing it even in the last six months of your life? Once you know that, then you can create a plan for introducing that job or those activities into your life.

Most of the people said that they would spend more time with the people they love. They would tell them they love them, that they appreciate them. Some said they would tell people they love that they are proud of them. If that was also your desire for the last six months of your life, start doing it now. Express those good feelings to people who you love and appreciate. Tell them that you love them. Tell them that they bring meaning into your life. You will make them happy, they would feel more loved, and you will feel more love for yourself, too.

Many people said that they would want to worry less about unimportant matters. They would also care less what other people would think of them. They would trust and have more faith that everything would be okay, that everything would be resolved. It was interesting to learn that before dying many people would want to focus more on what they wanted, not so much doing what other people would want or expect from them. Living their lives. Being braver. Taking more risks. Being who they are. They would be truly honest with themselves. In addition, many said they would want to take better care of themselves. Many would think more about their bodies, their eating habits, exercising, thinking positively, being healthy, and having more energy, so that the last six months they would really and truly experience life with all of their senses.

People would stop wasting time. Some people would write a book, write a note, and express something for their children, spouses, parents, friends, or the rest of the world to make this world a better place. Many people said they would quit watching the news, quit all the activities that are stealing precious time from them. They would spend more time in nature, more time moving, more time living. They would travel more, visit places, connect with different people, and spend time with friends from their childhood and friends that they have now. They would taste different foods, play more, dance more, listen to music, go to concerts of their favorite bands, do something crazy, different, being more playful and become like children again.

To me, based on what I learned doing this, I would summarize all the teachings from the book, based on my research done through my workshops and talking to people, to just four simple pieces of advice: spend more time with people you love, do what you love, make every moment count and be happy. Being happy is one of our deepest purposes as human beings. It is why you came to this planet and into this life.

When you love
someone, the best
thing you can offer is
your presence. How
can you love if you
are not there?

THICH NHAT HANH

SPEND MORE TIME WITH PEOPLE YOU LOVE

We take the people around us for granted. We also take time for granted. Many times we behave like we have unlimited time, and we procrastinate spending time with those people and in telling them we love them, etc. If we knew we were eating a last meal, a last supper with the people we sometimes take for granted, we would treat them nicely, with love, with compassion; we would talk to them and be fully present. So many times we sit at the same table, but our minds might be somewhere else. Or we might be stressed because of a particular situation at our jobs or simply because we had what we call a bad day and we are stressed out.

Often, we transfer or express stress to our loved ones. Knowing that this meal or this particular moment might be the last moment we have with a particular person, we would be gentler perhaps, more caring. Have you noticed how sometimes very old or ill people are treated? If you knew that perhaps a particular moment could be the last moment that we had with a person, we would certainly be more present for them. We would be forgiving, understanding, caring.

We would spend more time with our children if we were

aware of our imminent demise. Playing with them. Reading them bedtime stories. Talking to them and really listening to them. Being honestly interested in them as people. Trying to learn more about them. Being careful that when we say goodbye to them that day, we do it in a nice, gentle way, without any bad feelings and emotions. Forgive, ask forgiveness, be grateful for the people that are around you with all the imperfections they have. You have been given a new life. I encourage you, as a part of this book and these exercises, to spend more time with people you love and doing what you love, making every moment count.

One day you will
wake up and there
won't be any more
time to do the
things you've always
wanted. Do it now.

PAULO COELHO

DO MORE OF WHAT YOU LOVE DOING

It is funny how we get caught up in doing things we believe we must do. We do something because we get into a daily routine and we are simply in a comfort zone. We might do things because we were taught to do them. And we do not attempt doing things that we would like to do perhaps because of our limiting beliefs. We wish we could do something else, but we are afraid we might fail. Or we procrastinate as we falsely believe that we will do something tomorrow. And that tomorrow never comes. But the real gift of live is here and now. The only gift you have is now. Today. So use that gift to actually do what you love doing. Do what you love more.

If you do things that you love doing, time stops, you enjoy, you have fun. You may not know how to combine what you love doing with your job yet, but be creative. Look for opportunities. Learn, study, talk to the people who love what they do and are passionate about it. If you do not know what you love doing, go out and try different things. Find your purpose, your life's passion. Go out and create the life you want to create. You have everything you need to succeed and to create an incredible presence and magnificent new future. And never stop looking for that which you love doing. You will find it or it will find you. It will come naturally to you, like it did to me, just keep looking.

Some years ago, after I finished my studies, I never thought I would find my passion, what I truly loved. But speaking, being in front of people, inspiring them to improve their lives, creating new books, new audio or video materials to help and inspire people, feels so natural, so truly special. I now know it always was my life's purpose. And I know that there is something that you are really good at. Look at how you can convert that which you love doing, your passions, into something you could do for a living. Persist until you find something that you love doing and do it; you will never again have the feeling that you are really working. Find what you love doing, do what you love more and love what you do. Make your life spectacular.

I wanted to convince you that you must learn to make every act count, since you are going to be here for only a short while, in fact, too short for witnessing all the marvels of it.

CARLOS CASTANEDA

MAKE EVERY MOMENT COUNT

It is your life. Remember: yours and only yours. And your life is made out of those tiny, simple moments. Every single moment counts. Ensure that you do your best so that your life will count and every single moment you have is a special moment. So many people say that once they achieve their goals, they will be happy or they will enjoy life. Once something has been completed, like a mortgage payment or a loan, they will relax and enjoy life. It is like going to see a good movie, but throughout, just waiting for the movie to end because that would be the time to enjoy the movie. That should not be the reason we go to a movie. A movie-goer usually enjoys a film because of an unexpected emotional roller coaster. You like a good movie because it entertains you from the very first moment until the end. Every single moment in a movie counts. And that is how life is supposed to be. Remember: The rain is good, it helps plants to live and grow, and it brings water to the earth. It makes life better.

Remember to enjoy life all the way, to make those small moments from which life is made of count. Every single moment of your life should be cherished and enjoyed. Find ways in which you can make your small and special moments even happier. You can find excuses to celebrate for no reason at all.

You can be happy for no reason at all. Observe people, things, scenery. Do not be like people hiking to see a mountain peak, passing magnificent scenery, incredible nature, some breathtaking views, but simply ignoring all that and walking, looking, thinking only in the direction of the peak. Once they get there, they simply take a photo, show it proudly to friends and family; they made it, they have been to the peak and are already considering moving on to the next peak, next goal, next achievement.

That is what we all perhaps sometimes sadly do in different formats or contexts. We are too busy achieving, doing, working, worrying, solving, searching. We spend too much time in our heads, remembering or regretting some from the past, fearing something in the future. Doing it all, but making the moment count. It is very simply the lesson that I am about to share. Be happy here and be happy now. Every single moment of your life is unique. It cannot be repeated. It is unique and special. And your responsibility is to make it count. To enjoy it. To be present. To be grateful that you can experience it. To have loads of fun as life is supposed to be fun. Your main purpose on this planet is to be happy. Do what you love. Love what you do. Spend time with people you love. Love yourself. Love this magnificent planet and these magnificent people. Love the gift of life you have been given. Remember that you are in control of your mind. You are in control of how you feel. You are in control of your life. You can control the meaning that you give to a particular experience in your life. Decide to be happy.

Research has shown that the best way to be happy is to make each day happy.

DEEPAK CHOPRA

JUST BE HAPPY

It is simple. I hope, based on this book, you have further noticed it is stupid to worry about unimportant things. What a waste of time to be sad or angry about things that ultimately do not matter. I hope, based on this book, you discovered what is truly meaningful and important to you. Find it in your heart and your inner being to look for things that make you happy. Happiness is an activity. Therefore, I encourage you to do whatever you need to do to be happy. You came to this planet to enjoy life, to learn and discover new things, to meet wonderful people, different cultures, nationalities, try new foods, to visit places, etc. To have as many wonderful experiences as possible. Look for those new experiences. Help others to be happy. Get happy yourself. Do small acts of happiness for yourself.

The message of the entire book is to look at who and what is most important in your life and spend more time with those people. Do what you love and simply be happy.

I believe in you and I support you on your mission.

Create a long and happy life for yourself.

Just do and be happy.

With Love,
Aleksander Šinigoj

A FREE AUDIO RECORDING –
MY GIFT TO YOU

After you have purchased and read this book, you can download your free mind programming recording. It can help you experience similar exercises and the whole process of this book through the support of my voice and some additional questions.

You can download the link from: www.aleksandersinigoj. com/6monthstolive

The value of the recording is $97.00 USD. When you use the special promotional code, 6MONTHSTOLIVE, the amount will change to $0 USD and you will be able to download it free of charge. You will receive a link in your email account. Please verify your spam or junk mailbox in case the link goes there directly.
We recommend you use a headset or earphones for better effect. Do not listen to the recording while driving or operating any machinery, which requires your full attention. Only listen to the recording when you can relax completely.

ABOUT THE AUTHOR

Dr. Aleksander Šinigoj is an inspirational and motivational writer and speaker. His focus is on how to improve and change people's thinking and unconscious programming. His books have one common goal: touching and changing lives around the world. To absorb his books into the unconscious mind, he recommends reading his books more than once. He believes that in order to produce results in life, one must take action. But, in order to make good action-oriented decisions, actions must come from feelings that are both inspired and determined, rather than actions taken out of fear, greed or any other negative emotion. His books are about change, but not only change on the conscious level, but also the unconscious.

Procrastination, limiting beliefs, not expressing or using full potential and other unconscious limitations can block people from living the lives they dream about. When people change their unconscious programs, when they change their thoughts and feelings, they start to behave differently. When people behave differently they get different results. Accordingly, the unconscious change can bring better results to people. Dr. Šinigoj is now traveling the world and speaking to different organizations that would like to produce different results by changing the values, beliefs, strategies and behavior of their people. His fun, passionate, warm and mesmerizing method for presenting different topics makes his speeches and training workshops special, addictive and unique.

59991719R00103